Cool

PARKS
& TRAILS

Great Things to Do in the Great Outdoors

Katherine Hengel

**Checkerboard
Library**

An Imprint of Abdo Publishing
abdopublishing.com

abdopublishing.com

Published by Abdo Publishing, a division of ABDO,
PO Box 398166, Minneapolis, Minnesota 55439.
Copyright © 2016 by Abdo Consulting Group, Inc.
International copyrights reserved in all countries. No
part of this book may be reproduced in any form without
written permission from the publisher. Checkerboard
Library™ is a trademark and logo of Abdo Publishing.

Printed in the United States of America,
North Mankato, Minnesota
062015
092015

THIS BOOK CONTAINS
RECYCLED MATERIALS

Content Developer: Nancy Tuminelly
Design and Production: Jen Schoeller, Mighty Media, Inc.
Series Editor: Liz Salzmann
Photo Credits: Ad Meskens, Frankie and Maclean Potts,
Jen Schoeller, Shutterstock

The following manufacturers/names appearing in
this book are trademarks: Craft Smart®, Nice Ride
Minnesota®, Scribbles®, Sharpie®, Thompson's®
WaterSeal®

Library of Congress Cataloging-in-Publication Data
Hengel, Katherine.
  Cool parks & trails : great things to do in the great
outdoors / Katherine Hengel.
     pages cm. -- (Cool Great Outdoors)
  Includes index.
  ISBN 978-1-62403-698-9
  1. Outdoor recreation--Juvenile literature. 2. Natural
history--Juvenile literature. 3. Trails--Recreational use--
Juvenile literature. 4. Parks--Recreational use--Juvenile
literature. I. Title. II. Title: Cool parks and trails.
  GV199.5.H46 2016
  796.5--dc23
                    2014045317

To Adult Helpers:

This is your chance to inspire kids to
get outside! As children complete the
activities in this book, they'll develop new
skills and confidence. They'll even learn
to love and appreciate the great outdoors!

Some of the activities in this book will
require your help, but encourage kids to
do as much as they can on their own. Be
there to offer guidance when needed, but
mostly be a cheerleader for their creative
spirit and natural inspirations!

Before getting started, it helps to review
the activities and set some ground
rules. Remind kids that cleaning up is
mandatory! Adult supervision is always
recommended. So is going outside!

CONTENTS

Hike a Trail!

Hiking is a great way to explore the outdoors. It's an easy way to get some exercise. You don't need much more than your own two feet! Many parks have trails for hiking. But you can also just hike around your own neighborhood!

We spend most of our lives inside. Take a second to count the hours. You sleep inside. You eat inside. You study inside. That's life in the 21st century.

You've got to get out!

There are many ways to enjoy parks and trails. It's easy to learn how to be a prepared hiker. You can even play games! It all happens outside. And it's all good. They don't call it the great outdoors for nothing!

A NATURAL RECHARGE!

What's so great about the great outdoors? A lot! Being outside exposes us to the sun's natural light. The sun gives us **vitamin** D. Vitamin D keeps our bodies strong! Exposure to sunlight helps regulate our sleeping patterns. The more you are outside, the easier it is to fall asleep!

A Return to
NATURE & RECREATION

We go to different places for different things. Stores are for shopping. School is for learning. What are parks and trails for? Recreation!

Recreation can be anything you want it to be. Maybe you like bicycling or cross-country skiing. Maybe you enjoy exploring waterways or historic sights. Maybe you're just looking for somewhere to be with your friends. Parks and trails help you get outside to do what you like!

UNDERSTANDING

*P*arks are areas **designated** for human enjoyment. Some include buildings and playgrounds. Others are natural pieces of land for wildlife and nature preservation. Most parks in the United States are public and protected by law.

PARKS *at a Glance*

National parks are large areas maintained by the federal government. Yosemite National Park covers 1,189 square miles (3,081 sq km) in California.

State parks often preserve animal **habitats** and natural beauty. Bison roam Custer State Park in South Dakota.

Urban parks offer city residents much-needed green space. Central Park in New York City is a famous **urban** park.

PARKS & TRAILS

*T*rails are paths used for travel and recreation. You can find different trails in almost all parks. What's your favorite mode of **transportation**? Find a trail that's right for you!

TRAILS *at a Glance*

Cycling Trails

Check the air in your tires, and you're off!

Hiking Trails

Grab your hiking boots and travel on foot!

Cross-Country Skiing Trails

Bundle up and get outside!

Horseback-Riding Trails

Hit the trails with a four-legged friend!

PARKS & TRAILS

*H*ow do you find parks and trails? A really simple way is to ask around. Ask your parents and teachers. Ask your friends and neighbors. Or you can search online.

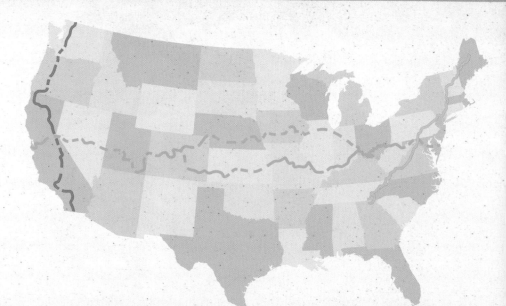

American Discovery Trail
- California to Delaware
- 4,834 miles (7,780 km) or 5,057 miles (8,138 km)

Pacific Crest Trail
- California to Washington
- 2,650 miles (4,265 km)

Appalachian Trail
- Georgia to Maine
- 2,200 miles (3,540 km)

ARE YOU READY?

1. Check the Weather
Check the forecast before you begin any outdoor adventure!

2. Dress Appropriately
Dress in layers! Be prepared for a **variety** of temperatures.

3. Bring Water
It's important to drink enough water, especially if it's hot out.

4. Get Permission
Some of the activities in this book require adult **supervision**. When in doubt, ask for help!

National Park Service
Information about all of the US national parks. **nps.gov**

National Trails System
Information about scenic, historical, and recreational trails. **nps.gov/nts**

America's State Parks
Information about parks in every US state. **americasstateparks.org**

Now let's get out and enjoy the great outdoors!

Materials

Here are some of the things you'll need.

acrylic paint

almonds

bike helmet

card stock

clear laminate

cashews

clear nail polish

dry-erase marker

dried cranberries

hair tie

hook-and-loop strips

hot glue gun & glue sticks

leaf

markers

measuring tape

needle

newspaper

nylon webbing

oilcloth

paintbrush

paper

peanuts

pinecones

plastic bottle

puffy paint

pen

rocks

scissors

shells

spray sealer

ruler

sticks

thread

tree bark

Pack It Up!

Make sure you have what you need on your hike. Grab a backpack and fill it with supplies. Here are some suggestions of things to bring along.

Cover Up

The weather can change quickly! Bring an extra layer to stay warm.

long-sleeved shirt

Water and Food

Stay full and **hydrated**!

water bottle

rain jacket

hat and gloves

healthy snacks
(try apples, granola bars, carrots, or trail mix)

Light the Way

Find your way even when it gets dark!

extra batteries

flashlight or headlamp

Navigation

Never get lost on your hike. Bring the right tools to help you get back!

GPS

map

compass

Emergency Kit

These items can help you stay safe and comfortable.

toilet paper

matches or lighter

insect repellant

whistle

first aid kit

knife

Sun Protection

Have a day of fun out in the sun! But make sure you don't get burned!

lip balm

sunscreen

sunglasses

REUSABLE
snack pack

Pack a sweet and savory snack for your next hike!

Materials

TRAIL MIX
1/2 cup dried cranberries
1/2 cup cashews
1/2 cup almonds
1/2 cup peanuts

SNACK PACK
ruler
oilcloth
scissors
thread
needle
hook-and-loop strips

1   Mix the trail mix ingredients together.

2   Cut a rectangle out of the oilcloth.
Make it 6 by 13 inches (15.2 by 33 cm).

3   Fold a short side up 6 inches (15.2 cm).
This leaves a little extra fabric for the flap.

4   Thread the needle. Sew one side together
from the bottom to the flap. Tie a knot in
the string. Sew the other side the same way.

5   Use scissors to round off the corners of
the flap. Cut a hook-and-loop strip 5 inches
(12.7 cm) long. Stick one side to the flap.
Fold the flap down. Stick the other strip
under the edge of the flap. The two strips
should line up.

6   Put the trail mix in the pack and you're
ready for a big hike!

MAGNIFICENT
walking stick

Materials

straight tree branch,
about 36 inches (91 cm) long
scissors
sandpaper
newspaper
acrylic paint
paintbrush
spray sealer

1 Cut any smaller branches off of the main branch.

2 Sand the branch until it is smooth. Wash it with water. Let it dry.

3 Cover your work surface with newspaper.

4 Paint the stick. Make different colored rings. Paint patterns on the stick. Let the paint dry.

5 Coat the stick with spray sealer to protect it.

Glue gems to your walking stick for extra bling!

hiking
BINGO

Materials

card stock
ruler
scissors
markers
clear laminate
dry-erase markers

1   Draw an 8-inch (20 cm) square on card stock. Cut it out. Divide it into a **grid** of 16 equal squares.

2   Draw something found in nature in each square. Examples include insects, flowers, leaves, trees, birds, and squirrels.

3   Cut two 9-inch (23 cm) squares of clear laminate. Peel the **backing** off one square. Lay it down with the sticky side up. Place the card stock on top of it.

4   Peel the backing off the second laminate square. Lay it on the card stock with the sticky side down. Smooth it out. Trim the laminate around the edges of the card stock.

5   Repeat steps 1 through 4 to make more bingo cards. Make sure they are all different.

6   Take the bingo cards on a hike. Mark off the items you see with dry-erase markers. Try to complete a row across, down, or **diagonally**.

no-hands water
HOLDER

Make a hands-free
hydration holder!

Materials

48 inches (122 cm) nylon webbing
clear nail polish
puffy paint
hair band
hot glue gun & glue sticks
water bottle

1   Paint the ends of the webbing with clear nail polish. This will stop them from wearing out. Let the polish dry.

2   Decorate the webbing with puffy paint. Let the paint dry.

3   Twist the hair band to make a double loop. Fold one end of the webbing around the hair band. Glue the fold in place.

4   Repeat step 3 with the other end of the webbing.

5   Slip the hair band around the neck of a water bottle.

natural
LAND ART

Create natural sculptures
on your hiking breaks!

Materials

wood bark
sticks
leaves
stones
pinecones
shells
rocks

Bark Boat

1   Collect a piece of soft, flat bark, a straight stick, and a large leaf.

2   Push one end of the stick gently through the middle of the bark. This is the mast.

3   Fold a leaf in half. Stick the mast through the leaf. Gently pull the leaf to the bottom of the mast. Float the boat on the water.

4   Take a picture of your artwork.

Simple Spirals

1   Collect small items such as stones, pinecones, and shells.

2   Find a flat surface. Arrange the items in a **spiral**. The spiral can be big or small.

3   Take a picture of your artwork.

Rock Stack

1 Collect some rocks. It could be just a few, or 20 or more.

2 Find a flat surface. **Stack** the rocks on top of each other.

3 Make more stacks. Try different arrangements. See how many you can stack!

4 Take a picture of your artwork.

TIP Only use things lying on the ground. Never pull branches, leaves, or flowers off of living plants.

bike helmet
MOHAWK

A ride in the woods
needs some fashion!

Materials

bike helmet
measuring tape
paper
pen
scissors
hook-and-loop strips
fuzzy cloth

1 Measure the helmet from back to front. Write down the measurement.

2 Cut two hook-and-loop strips the same length as the measurement.

3 Cut a piece of cloth 3 inches (7.5 cm) wide. Make it the same length as the helmet measurement.

4 Lay the cloth fuzzy side down. Peel the **backing** off one side of each hook-and-loop strip. Stick the strips to the cloth. Place them side by side.

5 Peel the remaining backing off of the hook-and-loop strips. Smooth the cloth over the helmet from back to front.

How Great Is the GREAT OUTDOORS?

Did you enjoy exploring parks and trails? Did any of the activities in this book inspire you to do more things in the great outdoors?

There is so much to love about being outside. These activities are just the beginning! Check out the other books in this series. You just might start spending more time outside than inside!

GLOSSARY

appropriately – in a manner that is suitable, fitting, or proper for a specific occasion.

backing – the paper that covers the sticky side of something, such as a stamp or sticker.

designate – to choose someone or something for a specific job or purpose.

diagonally – at an angle.

grid – a pattern with rows of squares, such as a checkerboard.

habitat – the area or environment where a person or animal usually lives.

hydrated – having enough water or moisture.

permission – when a person in charge says it's okay to do something.

spiral – a pattern that winds in a circle.

stack – 1. to put things in a pile. 2. a pile of things placed one on top of the other.

supervision – the act of watching over or directing others.

transportation – the act of moving people and things.

urban – of or related to a city.

variety – different types of one thing.

vitamin – a substance needed for good health, found naturally in plants and meats.

Websites

To learn more about Cool Great Outdoors, visit **booklinks.abdopublishing.com**. These links are routinely monitored and updated to provide the most current information available.

Index